SNOW STORM
MARKETING
COURSE

BY WARREN BROWN

ISBN 978-1-4457-3683-9

Publisher: Lulu Publishing

INTRODUCTION

The Snow Storm Marketing Course will guide you to developing, creating, producing and marketing your own products and services on an off the web. When you have followed the steps laid out here and have successfully created your own information or other product, you will be guided to advertising, making a mailing list and selling your products and services successfully, in the shortest possible time.

You possess the greatest fortune and yet you do not know it. Your wealth lies within you and it is in the form of your talent, which is waiting to be discovered. Now how would you go about discovering the talent that you have within you?.

We all have the potential to be Millionaires. No doubt a certain amount of luck is also necessary, for any venture which we attempt in life. This book will be a useful guide for those who are interested in becoming famous and rich. There is also hard work involved, as well as an investment into your own personality and abilities. I do hope that you enjoy this attempt of mine to present to you the reader, a comprehensive method to becoming famous and rich independently.

CONTENTS

1. Module 1   5
2. Module 2   10
3. Module 3   13
4. Module 4   16
5. Module 5   22
6. Module 6   25
7. Module 7   31
8. Module 8   39
9. Module 9   42
10. Module 10   49
11. Module 11   56
12. Module 12   65
13. Module 13   72
14. Module 14   76
15. Module 15   80
16. Module 16   88
17. Snow Storm Marketing Resources   111
18. About Warren Brown   114
19. Notes   115

MODULE 1

INTERNET MARKETING STRATEGIES

1. Web promotion and web site design.
2. SEO techniques in order to get a good search-engine ranking.
3. Email marketing
4. Using a suitable marketing niche, with the help of Affiliates, resellers and an Associate program.
5. Procuring advice from an Internet Marketing Coach or a Internet Consultant.
6. Building a responsive Opt-in Email List.
7. Publishing articles in Article Directories or as features in news stories.
8. Writing and publishing Press Releases online.
9. Sponsoring contests and free Giveaways through a website campaign.
10. Interacting with web visitors and customers by blogging, forums and social sites, such as Facebook and Twitter.

SHORT-TERM MARKETING STRATEGIES

1. Purchasing Advertising offline and online
2. Participating in Forums in your niche.
3. Search Engine submissions of your websites.

LONG-TERM MARKETING STRATEGIES

1. Opt-in List building
2. Blogging on your topic in your niche.
3. Social networking on social sites
4. Networking on Social bookmark sites

5. Giving away of Freebies on your sites, in order to generate a constant flow of traffic to your sites.
6. Article Marketing or the submission of articles to various article websites, on your topic.

WAYS TO MAKE MONEY ONLINE

1. Joining an Affiliate program, in order to sell Affiliate products.
2. Selling a service or your own product.
3. Selling of Electronic or Digital products
4. Creating a paid subscription or membership site.
5. Selling of physical products on the web, through online stores like EBay or CafePress.

SNOW STORM MARKETING BLUEPRINT

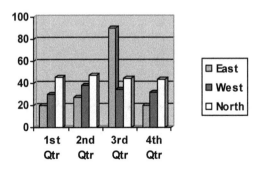

The Snow Storm Marketing Blueprint shows you the following three Essential Ingredients for this type of marketing to be effective and to generate a recurring income.

S	Site developed for a unique Niche
N	Networking on Social Sites
O	Original content, products in the form of ebooks, audios, courses, membership sites, subscriptions, forums, blogs
W	Writing Blogs, articles for Hubpages, Triond, Factoidz and article Directories
S	Search Engine Optimization, Squidoo sites, Social Bookmarks, Saturation of the market with the product or service
T	Targeting new niches with new products and services
O	Observation of new trends and the competitors
R	Recruiting Affiliates, members
M	Mailing list management, multiple product creation
MARKETING	Campaigns by Email, Advertising, Sponsorship and word-of-mouth

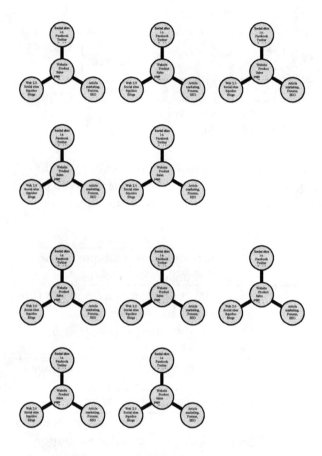

The Snow Storm Marketing Blueprint involves the following stages, MULTIPLIED SEVERAL TIMES, for Each and Every product that is released automatically.

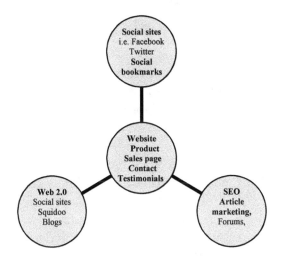

KEY ELEMENTS OF SNOW STORM MARKETING

1. Regular Product creation.
2. Updating of all sites and blogs
3. Constant Social Interaction, social sites, social bookmarks, forums
4. The giving away of Freebies to list members and to get new Affiliates
5. S.E.O. Search Engine Optimization
6. Press Releases for new products or any other features
7. Video casts for new products
8. Podcasts for new products and courses
9. Creating Multiple Streams of Income
10. Observation of new emerging trends in your Niche as well as exploring new areas of development in the marketplace.

MODULE 2

CREATE AND SELL YOUR OWN PRODUCTS

These are a few established print-on-demand sites which sell everything from t-shirts to clocks and from books to calendars and from fabrics to board-games. You can create and sell your own products.

1. CafePress- They have a large catalog of products, on which you can print logos and designs. CafePress offers hundreds of different products to sell, with a large community of users creating 45,000 new items each day.
2. Zazzle- This site offers a huge number of customizable products, with on-demand printing. Zazzle users have created more than 19.5 billion items online.
3. Spreadshirt- This site offers a very easy to use online product designer, which makes it simple for anyone to make, so that it can be sold in the open market.
4. Pikistore- This site offers a great store to create and sell products to the public and is worth visiting. You can sell customizable items, such as mugs, mouse-pads and t-shirts.
5. Lulu- Lulu offers a fantastic service for photographers and authors to publish printed book, CDs or DVDs. Lulu can help you to get your books listed on Amazon, Barnes and Noble and in bookstores as well.
6. Create Space- This site is owned by Amazon and offers authors, musicians and film-makers to create print-on-demand books, CDs and DVDs. You can also sell books on Kindle via the Amazon MP3 store.

7. Blurb- This site can produce great Photobooks and has attracted artists and photographers over the years. Blurb makes it simple to automatically create books with your content form Picasa, SmugMug, Flickr and TypePad.
8. TasteBook- This site produces great hardcover spiral bound cookbook binders which hold up to 100 recipes. Users can upload their own recipes or choos recipes from a large number of third-party providers.
9. CDBaby- There are over 200,000 indie artists who already sell their music through CDBaby. This company handles warehousing, selling and distribution of your CDs.
10. Game Crafter- On this site you can make and sell your own board games and collectible cards. All you need to do is upload your artwork, game rules and select which pieces (dices or pawns) need to be included. The Game Crafter will print, package and mail out the game every time it is ordered.
11. Spoonflower- This site is a print-on-demand fabric seller. It allows designers to create and sell printed fabrics, for various uses and at reasonable prices.
12. Ponoko- This site will take any 3D design and turn them into actual products, using a variety of materials such as cardboard, bamboo, leather, acrylic or felt. You can then make up your own toys, housewares, furniture, jewelry or electronics and sell them in your store online.
13. Shapeways- This is a site like Ponoko and lets you upload your 3D designs and turns them into real products using 3D technology. You can then sell your products through a customized store.

14. Imagekind- On this site artists can sell prints of their work. This site is owned by Café Press and specializes in prints and cards on a variety of materials.
15. DeviantArt- This is one of the largest art sites on the web, with over 81 million submissions. All artwork can be sold through the site's store printed on a variety of items from mugs to magnets.

AFFILIATE MARKETING BUSINESS

Affiliate marketing is all about selling the products online and getting commission on each such sale. Three best features about Affiliate Marketing are:

1. You don't need to have a product of your own.
2. You need not worry about technical support and customer complaints. The Product owner is responsible to the customer who has made the purchase.
3. You need not spend money to start. You can start affiliate marketing for free.

3 Steps of Affiliate Marketing

1. **Product Selection**
In order to succeed in affiliate marketing you will need to select a product, which belongs to a profitable niche. A product that suits your marketing style and at the same time is in demand will surely give you a great start. If you want a head start then you should select a product which you know a lot about. This will allow you to market your affiliate product more effectively.

2. **Landing Page Creation**
You will also need a high quality landing page with a good sales letter on display. Remember that the sales letter and the landing page play an important role to

increase the number of conversions. You should also make sure that you are building a list from your landing page as well. You can offer things like free eBooks etc in return for subscription. This will result in you having a powerful mailing list for your future product promotions.

3. Online Marketing
You should ideally market your products on all the fronts. You should use the paid advertisement and at the same time you should also try out the free methods. Some of the free methods are more beneficial than the paid advertisement.

It is easy to make money online especially from affiliate marketing but for this you need to do research into your niche and study the demand for the product.

MODULE 3

INFORMATION PRODUCTS

Information products include all books, reports etc. In the Internet context, the term refers to electronically deliverable, knowledge-based products.

Information products are also referred to as "digital goods" and "knowledge-based goods".

If your digital product delivers knowledge and you can e-mail it to the customer or offer it as a downloadable file, then it qualifies as an information product.

Information products can be created with little or no investment. Information products can be reproduced in any quantity - it is as simple as copying a file. Even if you sell a million copies, your production costs stay at zero.

TYPES OF INFORMATION PRODUCTS

E-books
E-zines and e-newsletters
Reports and research data
Tutorials, courses & Guide books.

HOW TO CREATE YOUR OWN INFORMATION PRODUCTS

1. Demand- A topic which people are interested in knowing more about.
2. Quality- The product needs to be of the best quality.
3. Presentation- The presentation of the product should be of a high standard, with a good cover image and powerful content.
4. Repeat Business- Create a long-term business plan and ask customers to return for upgrades and updates to the product they have purchased.
5. Legal Issues- Always do a trademark check on the title of your information product, before launching it in the marketplace.

THREE ESSENTIAL STEPS TO CREATE A KILLER PRODUCT

1. **Research-** Collect all the information you can on the Niche you are interested in. In order to know for sure if you are heading in the right

direction, do some surveys, customer research, as well as the all important Keyword research.

2. **Format-** Decide on a proper format for your e-book or digital product.
3. **Create-** Go ahead and create your killer digital product, while giving it the zing factor, which will make your customers want to have it.

INTERNET MARKETING TOOLS

1. Viral Marketing- Generating interest in a product or service by blogging, social networking and article marketing.
2. Videocasts- Creating short videos for You Tube, Metacafe or other video sites on the web.
3. Podcasts- Distribution of your audio content on the web.
4. Blogging on web about your product or service.
5. Affiliate Marketing- The selling of other people's products for a commission.
6. Email Marketing to your list of customers.

ARTICLE DIRECTORIES

1. EZINE ARTICLES
   http://www.ezinearticles.com

2. IDEA MARKETERS
   http://www.ideamarketers.com

3. GO ARTICLES
   http://www.goarticles.com

4. ARTICLE UNDERGROUND
   http://www.articleunderground.com

MODULE 4

INCLUDE FAME AND FORTUNE IN YOUR NEW YEAR RESOLUTIONS

a. It should be interesting

b.. It should not be too time consuming

c.. It should be something which you had wanted to do for some time

d. It should be realistic

e. It should be achievable by you

f. It should be humanly possible

g. You should be willing to ask for assistance in order to achieve this goal.

h. You should be willing to inform your family and friends about your New Year resolutions, if it involves them, so that they can support you in fulfilling your objective

i. You need to be enthusiastic about this resolution

j. You should be willing to set aside time in order

to achieve this objective

k. You should be willing to accept defeat or failure in achieving this goal, yet to be able to learn from this experience

l. You need to reward yourself after the successful achievement of your resolution. Celebrate your accomplishment

m. Get inspiration and motivation in order to keep you focused throughout the year.

n. Learn from your mistakes and make them learning experiences.

o. Assist others in accomplishing their goals and resolutions

p. Decide that you will do something outstanding this year. You need to reveal your hidden talent to the world.

q. Make a few Videos and put them on to You Tube. In no time you will find that you have your own fan following.

AFFILIATE MARKETING: THE AMAZON STORE

Join Amazon.com as an Affiliate and start promoting your Online Store, on your websites and blogs. You will also need to open a Pay Pal account so that all your Affiliate Commissions can be sent to your account. You can also invest some money is Advertising online and offline so that more people visit your Store. Start by sending all your friends, contacts and family your Store URL, so that they can visit your store. Next you will need to submit your Store URL to as many Search-Engines as possible. I have just successfully opened a new Amazon Store. You are welcome to visit the store and find some exciting gifts with some great offers.

http://astore.amazon.co.uk/warrbrowlitee-21

SOCIAL NETWORKING: FACEBOOK AND TWITTER

I have joined Facebook and Twitter, in order to promote my work. Both social networking sites have a lot of rules, so you must make sure that you follow all the rules and do not get banned from the sites. Sokule is another great site you can join and promote your products or services, without the fear of getting banned from using the site.

GETTING TAGGED ON FACEBOOK

It is a great way to get noticed, when you are Tagged on Facebook. Getting Tagged on Facebook is yet another way of getting your work spotted. I was tagged on Facebook sometime ago, see the list below:

1. I enjoy creative writing articles, blogs, stories, poetry and reading non-fiction.
2. I like cooking Anglo-Indian dishes, as prepared by my Mum, as well as experimenting with exciting Chinese and Indian preparations as well.
3. I like reading the American Superhero comics.
4. I love the movies. American movies of all genres. Indian movies: historical and period pieces. British movies based on the classic novels, as well as the old comedies, like the Carry On series and the TV series "Jeeves & Wooster" and "Black Adder". I love watching comedies and having a hearty laugh.
5. I am deeply interested in Dreams, mysticism and the meaning of Symbols in Art and Architecture.
6. I am also interested in the Paranormal like UFOs, extra-terrestrials and the Unexplained.
7. I enjoy the medium of the web and have been working on the web since 1998.
8. I think that there is great potential in Ecommerce and we are just at the beginning of a renaissance in the Golden Age of Internet Marketing.
9. I am a trained Life Coach and I enjoy helping others to excel and to be a Success in their field of endeavour.
10. I am interested in Copywriting and I have done a Copywriting course from American Writers and Artists Incorporate.
11. I love my family, family matters a lot to me, from my wife, to my Mum(who passed away recently), my Dad, my sister, my brother-in-law, my two nieces, my nephew, my relatives in India, Australia and Canada.
12. I value my friends and my network of people who enjoy reading my work and supporting my various causes, both on and off the web.
13. I love marketing for fresh vegetables, this was due to the fact that Mum and I would do a lot of marketing while growing up.
14. I love watching the rain, mum and I loved to watch the pouring rain, except when it was lightning and Mum

would run back into the room. Rain nourishes the soil and brings with it new life.

15. I enjoy photography, video filming and have prepared a number of short videos. I also like script-writing and directing of short films.

16. I really like the world of Publishing and I have been involved with printing and publishing since a very young age and my Dad has been actively in print media. I have published a lot of my work on the Lulu self publishing site. I am also a Publishing Consultant helping everyone who wants to be a Writer to prepare and publish their own work, with minimum investment.

17. I was a librarian for over eleven years at the Goethals Indian Library and Research Society in Calcutta, India. I have the traits of a Librarian and Researcher, which is an added advantage for a writer and publisher on the web. At present I am an Administrator in London.

18. I have a number of philosophies about life, like we are all here for a purpose, that this is not the end and whatever we do at the beginning of our life will be repeated on in later years in a more magnified way.

19. I Believe in Miracles and in the Power of the individual to make a positive difference in the World.

20. I enjoy website making and Affiliate Marketing, especially pasting the HTML code onto a website and watching it take on a whole new life, when it is published on the web.

21. I find courses on different subjects very fascinating which is why, I have successfully completed different courses over the years. I have completed a number of courses like "Advertising and Public Relations", "Teachers Training", "Library Science", "Entrepreneurship Development Programme", "Computer Science", "Life Coaching", "The Effective Administrator" and "The AWAI Copywriting Program".

22. The Indestructible Soul: I Believe that the Soul is indestructible based on the Law of Energy, "that energy is neither created nor destroyed, as it is transformed from one form to another, while remaining constant throughout". We all have to go back to where we came from and our Soul is energy.

23. Movies of Special significance for me are given below:

(a) Superman with Christopher Reeve

(b) Sound of Music my Mum's favourite movie

(c) James Bond, with Roger Moore.

(d)Tarzan movies (Johnny Weismuller and with Christopher Lambert) which I would go and see with my Dad.

(e) The Bud Spencer and Terence Hill movies

(f) The Sherlock Holmes series with Jeremy Brett

(g) Silverado

(h) Batman

(i) Star Wars

24. I Believe, that it is important in life to have an opinion on everything and to search for information on everything that you find interesting in life. I guess that it is my natural librarian instinct.

25. Take the time to appreciate and record your life, as a source of inspiration and encouragement for your future and to inspire others with your example.

MODULE 5

MAKE YOUR OWN NING NETWORKS

Creating your Ning Networks is yet another superb method for sending more traffic to your sites and blogs, where you are displaying and selling your products and services. I you specialize in collecting and selling old books and comics, then it would be a great idea for you to create a comic and rare book network on Ning, where you can assist others, with your own specialized knowledge as well as promote your products.

If you happen to be a singer, with a number of your songs recorded on CDs. You can always create a site devoted to selling your own music videos and CDs. Create a Ning network with your music as your theme, giving free sample downloads of your music, as well as sending your members to your website or blog, where your CDs and DVDs are sold.
Super heroes Comics on Ning

http://superheroescomics.ning.com/

Romance Unlimited on Ning

http://romanceunlimited.ning.com/

Understanding Dream Symbols and Dream Interpretation

http://dreamology.ning.com/

Guiding You to a Successful Life

http://lifecoachingunlimited.ning.com/

Money Making Ideas and Web Marketing

http://moneywebmarketing.ning.com/

Making Poetry work for you Positively

http://poetrytherapy.ning.com/

BOOK PUBLISHING

If you have an innate talent for writing, then I would advise you strongly to start writing seriously now. This is the best time to write and publish your own books, with minimum investment. Your product will be the books that you publish. You can buy a dot com website to promote your book and your writings.

A Romantic Time for Rhyme and Success Poetry by Warren Brown

The Amazon Book Store Listing

Permalink: http://amzn.com/1409285421

Buy Your Copy from the Lulu Bookstore-UK

The Lulu Bookstore

http://stores.lulu.com/warrenmelvynbrown

£11.43
Ships in 3–5 business days

This is a collection of seventy-five poems, written by
Warren Brown, winner of the "Henry Louis Vivian
Derozio", Anglo-Indian Poetry Award, on a variety of
subjects, from Robin Hood, Britain's got Talent,
Superheroes, to Ninjas and Shoguns, Elvis Presley, the
Boxer and "London Historica" or The History of
London. Discover the art of Poetry Therapy and also
uncover the poems on success and positive living. This
collection of poems is the perfect gift for anyone who
wishes to discover the curative powers of poetry.

PUBLISHING ON AMAZON KINDLE

If you have written a number of Reports or ebooks on an topics of interest, the you can publish them on Amazon Kindle. There is a demand for ebooks on almost every Niche. Do some research on a niche which you find interesting, check the demand for it on the web, using a bit of keyword research. Write an ebook or report on your niche. Next join the Kindle Author publishing program and upload your work. Before long you will receive a link to your ebook from Kindle.
Kindle Codes for my Four Books on Kindle at present:
B003BEDV0S
B003BEDW5C
B003BEDW98
B003ARTKTC

MODULE 6

SEARCH-ENGINES: These search-engines are of vital importance for any form of e-commerce on the web. It is always good to know how the system works and to make an attempt to get your websites and blogs listed on some of these powerful search-engines. There are thousands of search-engines on the web, the most powerful being Google, Yahoo and now Bing.

Search Engine Optimization and Keywords are essential in all the Copywriting that you do to promote your products and services on the web. I have found that the WEB CEO program, which is a free tool which works to submit your websites and blogs to Search-Engines world-wide is very effective.
I get a lot of traffic from all over the world. The WEB CEO program has a free and a paid version as well. It will help you to understand the nature and the value of

Keywords and how it works to get a website on the top listings, as well as to drive traffic to a site. SEO (Search Engine Optimization) is very interesting and it worth taking some time to understand.

SEO COPYWRITING ESSENTIALS

1. Create an appropriate Theme related to the Niche of your website.
2. Keyword Research related to your site is vital.
3. Create useful content related to your Niche site.
4. Title Tags are useful for your web articles.
5. Placement of Keywords should be done carefully for maximum exposure.
6. Keywords need to be strategically placed in your content.
7. Synonyms of Keywords should be used.
8. Meta Tags need to be entered onto the site and within the content.
9. Images should be used instead of text.
10. Originality of content is extremely essential.
11. The Whole Site needs to be Optimized for best results.
12. Link your site to other related Niche sites.
13. Maintain a proper Word Count for your articles.
14. Keywords should be used at appropriate sections in your content.
15. An Effective Landing Page needs to be planned, created and developed.
16. Statistics related to your site, like web visitors and Tags need to be studied and analyzed.
17. Create Back-links to your Content, which link to other related content on other locations or to other websites and blogs.

FOREX ON THE WEB

Foreign Exchange refers to the buying and selling of foreign currency. There have been a number of FOREX Millionaires who have made their fortunes with foreign exchange.

I have listed a few of the Definitions of Foreign Exchange for your interest:
Definitions of FOREX on the Web:

• The foreign exchange market (currency, forex, or FX) is where currency trading takes place. It is where banks and other official institutions ...
http://en.wikipedia.org/wiki/FOREX

• Foreign Exchange
http://en.wiktionary.org/wiki/forex

• The foreign exchange market, where brokerage firms and banks are connected over an electronic network that allows them to convert the currencies ...
http://investor.infospaceinc.com/tr/glossary.cfm

• The simultaneous buying of one currency and selling of another.
http://www.trading-futures-markets.com/glossary.htm

• An over the counter market where buyers and sellers conduct foreign exchange transactions.
http://www.aibcm.com/servlet/ContentServer

• Forex is short for foreign exchange. When one speaks of a forex profit or loss, he is talking about the increased or decreased value of an ...
http://www.garyascott.com/currez/glossary.html

• Foreign Currency Exchange

http://www.greekshares.com/forex_terms.php

• Any type of financial instrument-from electronic transactions to paper currency, checks, and signed, written orders called bills of exchange

http://www.morganstanleyindividual.com/customerservice/dictionary/Default.asp

• The international exchange market, the market for conversion exchange operations of specified amounts of one country's currency into the currency of another country according to an agreed rate for a given date.

http://www.forexltd.co.uk/resources/glossary

• Any type of financial instrument that is used to make payments between countries is considered foreign exchange. ...

http://www.pathtoinvesting.org/dictionary/words_f.ht m

FOREX TUTORIAL, GLOSSARY AND BASICS

WATCH ETORO HIGH VALUE VIDEOS AND TUTORIALS
http://www.etoro.com/A15345_TClick.aspx

FOREX TUTORIAL
http://www.investopedia.com/university/forexmarket/ forex1.asp
http://www.forexyard.com/en/forex-tutorial

FOREX GLOSSARY
http://www.forexyard.com/en/glossary

FOREX BASICS
http://forextrading.about.com/od/forexbasics/a/what _is_forex.htm

FOREX PRODUCTS

Real Money Doubling FOREX Robot

http://budurl.com/ar6m

FOREX Mega Droid works to bring you Money

http://budurl.com/uygb

Live FOREX Videos

http://budurl.com/ffut

Profit with Accurate FOREX Signals

http://budurl.com/u47m

FOREX Auto-pilot keeps bringing you the Profits

http://budurl.com/p7h4

MODULE 7

OPENZINE ARTICLES

Openzine is a very innovative Ezine on which you can publish your photos, videos and articles on your specialized subject. Creating your own Ezine on Openzine is another way of getting more people to read your work and this is another method for driving more traffic to your site or blog, on which you sell your products. On Openzine you can put all your writings on a particular Niche (area of interest), for an issue. This is one way of exploring and showing your expertise in different fields. If you are recognized as an Expert in a certain field, it will not be long before people are willing to listen to you and to purchase your products and services.

Answers to Life in Poetry Therapy

Poetry reading and writing has always been of great interest to many over the years, the decades and the centuries. Poetry has been respected as a literary Art all over the world, in all cultures, heritages and languages.

Poetry has undergone great transformations over the years. The poets of today stand tall on the shoulders of those great poets like, William Shakespeare, William Wordsworth, Henry W. Longfellow, Emily Dickinson, William Blake, Wilfred Owen and Shelley, whose poems and writings are immortal and have an impact in shaping the destiny of mankind.

Discovering the Art of Poetry

One of the best ways to discover the art of poetry writing is to visit the library and to read the work of some of the greatest poets who have walked the Earth. Next, it would be a good idea to study the structure and the pattern of the various types of poems, from Romantic poetry to Nature poems and from epics and ballads to sonnets, elegies, odes and epigrams. The 16th century Japanese Haiku and the new free verse of modern society are two examples of the evolution of poetry.

Listening to poems can help to put you into a poetic frame of mind, while helping you to appreciate the beauty and the structure of the poems.

Reading poems can help you to feel the rhythm of the poems and appreciate the manner in which the poet has treated his subject.

Writing poetry is a great experience in itself. The three stages in writing a poem of value would be to capture an idea, visualize the thought, select a few words related to the concept, with a ring to them and then proceed to develop your idea in the form of verse. Try creating couplets, if you are good at rhyming and then start to create a style following a pattern of poems you have read. But, if you like freedom, try writing your poem in free verse.

Experiencing Poetry in your life

The best way to experience poetry is to think and feel like a poet. See the beauty in everything around you. Know that all life is connected. Read the work of the great poets and visualize all the powerful images and feelings which they have invoked within you.

Every little idea has the potential to become a powerful poem, with the right words and the right meaning giving it life.

Poetry Therapy for Success in Life

I have found the writing of poetry very therapeutic. Poetry gives you the opportunity to express your feelings in words and images. It also gives you a chance to put words to all the ideas which come to your mind and which would be lost forever, if they are not put to some creative use.

When you feel unhappy read or listen to an audio poem which can help you to alleviate your mood and make your day more pleasant.

When you are happy about some new event occurring in your life or in the world around you, take some time to put your feelings of the moment into a few lines. I find that it is a challenge to be able to put a big idea into a few lines of verse.

When you are looking for a challenge, take the time to write a poem on a boring subject, and make it a poem, to grab the interest of your reader. I practised writing poems based on historical fact, to make it more interesting and mentally appetizing for a reader.

A poem is an excellent way to channel your creative talents. You can create a poem which may seem frivolous today, but which at sometime or for someone else have a deeper meaning. Make an attempt at trying your hand at writing all types of poems. It is always best to let your thoughts flow when you are writing poetry. This is one of the best ways for releasing your creativity.

There have been times when I have written more than five poems in a day. It was just that the ideas started flowing, and there came a time when the poetry would write itself. What do I mean by saying that a poem would write itself? This means that the words, the images, the rhyme and the rhythm would all fall into place seemingly by magic once I had a concrete image or concept in my mind about the concept I wanted to write about. I have been writing poems from the age of seventeen, my first poem being, "The Lady of the Sea". Since that poem I have not looked back. I do hope that you find the writing of Poetry as enjoyable and therapeutic as I do. I would like to wish you all the best for your future endeavours in writing poems for yourself, your family and the poetry lovers of the world.

URL: http://www.openzine.com/aspx/Zine.aspx?IssueID=4116
Publish Success on Openzine
www.openzine.com/publishsuccess

Making a Good Living with Laughter Therapy

"Laughter is the best Medicine" and the best antidote to sadness and unhappiness. If you love to laugh you will discover that you do feel better after having a good hearty laugh. Laughter at anything we find funny or tickles our funny bone is also a good way to relieve stress. Keeping this point in mind, a number of laughter clubs have been created over the years.

We all laugh in a different way. Some of us "laugh through our noses, while some of us laugh through our teeth hissing and thissing like snakes", we should love to laugh. I find that it is an excellent way to relax. Do not be embarrassed of laughing out loud, if that happen to be the way you like to laugh.

I remember the time when my parents, sister and I would go to the movies when we were growing up. I loved the comedies because they would really make me laugh. I remember watching the Charlie Chaplin movies, the Norman Wisdom movies, the Crazy Boys movies, and having a loud hearty laugh in my seat. Mum and Dad would tell me to quieten down sometimes, as I would occasionally be the only person in the cinema hall having a good laugh.

The dinner table family conversations were also times when we would all have a good laugh. Those were memorable times when my Mum, Dad, sister and I would sit around the table chat about the events during the day and have a good laugh. Mum would wipe away her tears, as she would laugh at the jokes I would share. I have always loved humour and wit growing up, and the family dining table was the one place where I would practise to sharpen my wit and satire. Later on in years, after my marriage, Mum, Dad, my wife and I would sit around the same table and share jokes and laugh at life in general. Those were all the happy memories I can remember today, those are the thoughts which bring Mum back to me in my mind. Mum passed away a few months ago and I miss her very much. Laughter, humour and happiness are the ingredients of happy memories whenever we need to remember our loved ones.

Take time to laugh today and if you are not in the habit of doing so, learn the art of humour and wit and get to know the secret recipe to enjoying life. Is there room in your life for humour and laughter? Like in the words of that great Comedian, Peter Sellers, in the Pink Panther, as Inspector Clouseau, "Do you have a rooooom?".

I thoroughly enjoyed watching the antics of Peter Sellers and Charlie Chaplin as they brought the screen and my humour alive whenever they tumbled onto the silver screen. Take time to Laugh your socks off today, it could even add a few years to your life. Laugh at life and laugh at yourself and before long you could be laughing your way to the bank, if you make laughter a skill and laugh your way into the International Comedy circuit and maybe even Hollywood. You could have another Jim Carrey or Robin Williams lurking somewhere in your comic nature. Take time to have a laugh today.

MODULE 8

Life Coaching Niche

It is truly rewarding when you can help a person to get control of his or her life. A Life Coach should always be close at hand to help an individual to understand, solve and create a plan to gain a better perspective into life's challenges. There are times in life when we feel that we are truly burdened with life's problems, we feel we are like Atlas holding the world on our shoulders. You need not worry any longer. There is that one person who can help you to better understand your life situation, to know your place and your role in your life, that valuable individual is your guide and mentor, your Life Coach.

Life has so much to offer each and every one of us. We all share common problems, but the unique way in which we are built changes our reactions to our life situations.

We all have unique personalities, we grow up in different life situations, we are all genetically unique, but, at the same time, we must remember, we are all part of the human race.

We all should have goals in life, in order to feel the need to get up every morning with a purpose in life and to go to sleep every night with a feeling of having done something worthwhile at night. We all do not have great jobs and we all do not have perfect relationships or have freedom from financial worries. With the help of a Life Coach we can overcome our fears about our relationship, financial or career worries, while we are encouraged to develop self motivation for success.

The main role of a Life Coach is to help you to better understand the forces which are working in your life, and to help you to gain an understanding into your personality and the effect you have on the world around you. You can be your own Life Coach, once you have achieved that level of understanding, so that we do not have to be victims of our life situations, instead we will be able to control and plan our lives for the sweet stink of Success.

Life Coaching Unlimited Network

What are the benefits of Joining this new Life Coaching Network?

1. Find out about Life Coaching and benefit from the knowledge.

2. Learn how you can resolve your issues in life.

3. Learn valuable skills to handle different life consultations.

4. Get Free Advice from a Certified Life Coach, Warren Brown.

5. Learn how you can reach your full potential in Life.

6. Share your thoughts, ideas, opinions, photos and videos on this Life Coaching network.

Success Life Coaching on the Openzine Publish Success

URL:
http://www.openzine.com/aspx/Zine.aspx?IssueI D=2527

MODULE 9

ARTICLE MARKETING ON THE WEB

Writing and submitting articles on various topics (Niches), is another method for establishing yourself as an Expert in a particular field as well as to drive more traffic to your sites and blogs. This is referred to as Article Marketing, as requires a bit of hard work, as you will need to churn out several dozens of article a week, in order to constantly be seen by readers and visitors to the article sites. In several case, Marketers employ freelancers to write for them on a particular Niche, so that they do not need to put in all the hard work. There are also Marketers who purchase PLR (Public Label Rights) to specialized Niches. Public Label Rights are packs of articles on particular topics, to which you are given exclusive rights to use as your own. These articles are either turned into e-books, courses, newsletters or used also for audio recordings and webinars etc.

NICHE: HONEY

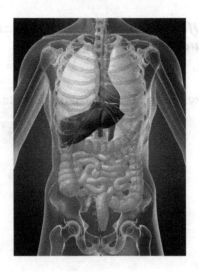

Honey Cures Health Problems

Honey has a number of medicinal uses and is beneficial for infants and adults. Honey is also helpful in weight control. A spoonful of honey can take away a number of health problems.

It has been proved over the years that honey has a number of useful medicinal uses. For example, one to three teaspoons of honey can cure stomach problems, such as acid indigestion. In the noted medical journal "Lancet", Doctors have also referred honey for the treatment of ulcers.

As a wound healer, honey can work miracles as it is rich in sugar, enzymes, vitamins, minerals and other nutrient factors. When honey is applied topically to wounds it heals them faster. Honey does not only disinfect the wound, but also repairs the area and is found to be more effective than expensive hospital wound dressings.

It has also been recommended over the years that honey should be used in infant formulas, to provide a wholesome sweetener, supplementary minerals, an antiseptic and a mild laxative for babies. Honey has a definite beneficial influence on calcium retention in infants.

In order to maintain the right weight it is necessary to monitor your sugar intake. It has been noticed after scientific observations that honey used as a sweetener does not result in heavy production of body fat, like refined sugar does. Honey is palatable, digestible as well as nutritious for the human body.

Large numbers of nutrition experts consider honey to be a source of good nourishment for the "power supply" of the vital heart muscle, upon which athletes have a greater dependence when training.

Honey has a number of interesting uses, from being used as a laxative, for facial treatment, as a face lotion, an antiseptic or antibiotic, for facial softening, as a facial scrub, as a cure for Diarrhoea, for bed-wetting treatment to being used as a cough syrup, elbow rub softener, burn cure and as a sore throat remedy. Keep a bottle of honey at home and soon you will be able to cure your common ailments, with a spoonful of honey.

http://healthmad.com/alternative/honey-cures-health-problems/

Use Nature's Pharmacy for Good Health

This article focuses on three natural foods found in nature which are good for your health. These simple and easy to obtain natural gifts of nature are Honey, Garlic and Vinegar.

In nature we can find a number of things which are good for our health. But, there is a special collection of three of nature's gifts to mankind which are Honey, garlic and vinegar. Honey is one of nature's sweetest food and is created by the bees who work tirelessly to produce this special preparation.

The second and one of the most powerful healing herb and spice of great flavour, which also happens to be a nourishing vegetable is the humble garlic. The third on the list we find Vinegar, which represents nature's most potent and versatile fermented food, with a number of beneficial uses to man.

The common factors of these three natural gifts to man from nature are that they are easy to find, cheap to buy and are widely available in all countries and in all types of weather conditions. All three foods, garlic, honey and vinegar are known to be extraordinary healing agents, present in all types of natural healing methods, such as folk medicine, which has been used for centuries.

Garlic, honey and vinegar are safe and versatile when used to heal particular ailments and they also seem to cure unrelated problems. Unlike the use of prescription medicine, these natural foods can be used without presenting any great health risks. It has been said that if your body is taken care of, it could provide you with excellent health for 80 to 120 years. In order to attain this level of health, there are four aspects of your life you need to take special care of. The four keys to a healthy body are a proper diet, suitable exercise, a positive attitude and to monitor your exposure to toxins in your food and those toxins which are present in your home and work environment. Take care of your health and body today and you could live till you are a hundred and four.

http://healthmad.com/health/use-natures-pharmacy-for-good-health/

Bees: The Marvels of Nature

The bee is a truly remarkable creature with a unique body structure which defies the principles of aeronautics. The bee is also the creator of such important products like bee's wax, honey, bee pollen and royal jelly.

The tiny buzzing bees are true marvels of nature. Scientists have studied the flight of bees and have noticed that according to their body structures, it should be impossible for them to fly based on the principles of aeronautics. Yet, the bees fly effortlessly in the air. Bees also happen to be along with silkworms the only domesticated insects on the planet. The hard working bees create vast reserves of bee's wax, honey, bee pollen and royal jelly.

If bees cease to exist or do become extinct, then we would lose about 2.2 billion pounds of annual honey production around the world. It has also been noticed in studies that without the cross pollination of bees during their pollen and nectar gathering, at least 90 species of fruits, vegetables and grains would die out.

Bees have found a vital place in history itself. Thanks to the existence of bees the phrase, "love as sweet as honey, has been coined, as well as the inclusion of wax candles to light up the night in ancient times and even the preparation of wax moulds to make gold, over the centuries.

http://scienceray.com/biology/zoology/bees-the-marvels-of-nature/

MODULE 10

COMMUNITY NICHE

THE SECRET RACE ON PUBLISH SUCCESS OPENZINE

In this Issue of Openzine, I have made the theme the Anglo-Indian community. This is yet another Niche which I use to promote my works on the web. I have created a number of videos and other related products, on the Anglo-Indian community.

THE ANGLO-INDIAN POEM BY WARREN BROWN

In sixteen hundred
British merchants came.
Soldiers followed for
adventure and fame.

The traders now set up
four colonies
To implement the trade
Charter policies.

When Britons took
native girls for their brides
All the girls parents
would cast them aside.

The outcast lady's issue
would now be
An Anglo-Indian in History.

In the past our Heroes were
Sir Gidney and James Kyd.
Now, they are Norman Hutchinson
and Peter Sarsted.

The next generation
steps in with their sole mission,
To fulfill, the Anglo-Indian Vision.

Remembering Anglo-Indian Heroes by Warren Brown

Every race on the planet takes pride in its Heroes and its Legends. From Genghis Khan, Aurangzeb, Shivaji to Oliver Cromwell, human civilization has brought forth its heroes, during times of fear and oppression, for people to follow, aspire to and emulate. The Anglo-Indian community also has its share of courageous soldiers and adventurers who fought in several wars down the ages.

In 1916 at least 8,000 Anglo-Indians had joined various British units, a large number were enlisted in the Dorset Regiment. The Cavalry and the Royal Artillery attracted the Anglo-Indians more than the Infantry. However, their records of identity and gallantry were lost to the community.

On the 15th March 1916, the authorities sanctioned the raising of an Anglo-Indian force as an integral part of the British army. The Anglo-Indian legend, James Skinner who was also referred to as Sikander Sahib, was born in 1775. His mother was a Rajput and his father a Scotsman. He and his "yellow boys", were freelance soldiers and fought for a number of Rajahs. During battle they would wear yellow shawls , hence the origin of their nickname.

Skinners irregular cavalry, called "Skinners' Horse", turned out to be one of the finest regiments of the British and later the Indian Army. He was decorated with the "Knight of the Order of the Bath".

James Skinner died at the age of 64 in 1841.In 1978 the Indian Government issued a postage stamp to celebrate 175 years of the Skinners' Horse Regiment.

During the Sepoy Mutiny of 1857, essential services like the Post and Telegraphs, the Railways and Customs were manned by Anglo-Indians.
The Gardner's Horse, founded by Colonel William Linnaeus Gardner is one of India's proud regiments today. William Gardner was gazetted as an Ensign in the 18th Foot on the 7th March, 1793.

He was the eldest son of Major Valentine Gardner who was the elder brother of Alan, First Lord Gardner . William was a skilled rider and swordsman.

He was held in very high esteem by both Indians and Europeans. In 1804 it appears that Gardner was in the service of the Raja of Jaipur. He later joined the British and started the Cavalry Corps , known as the "Gardner's Horse".He is described as a gentleman and a soldier.

Gardner died at his estate at Khasgunj, at the age of 65, on the 20th July
1835. His wife died of a broken heart six months later. His wife was a princess and he had two sons and a daughter from her. Colonel Henry Forster, was the son of Henry Pitts Forster of the East India Company's Civil Service who came out to India in1783.

Henry Pitts Forster was later made the Master of the Calcutta Mint. Henry Forster was born in 1793, and being of mixed descent he was disqualified from obtaining service in the Company.

 Finally he joined the Mahratta Army, and in 1816 he was appointed Adjutant of the second regiment of Skinner's Horse. During the outbreak of the Mutiny, Forster was detailed to reduce the mutinous 34th N.I. and Ramghur Infantry in Singhboom, Manbhoom and Chaisbasa. Having accomplished this Forster was ordered to perform a similar task at Sumbulpore. On his arrival, he was appointed Commissioner. Colonel Forster died at his residence in Calcutta, at Ballygunge, after a prolonged attack of fever, in 1862. Colonel Forster first married Miss Kellner who was murdered at Delhi, during the Mutiny. His second wife was an Indian lady.

Major Hyder Young Hearsey, was the son of a Jat lady by Captain Henry Hearsey. By coincidence he was given the name of Hyder, who was one of England's greatest enemies, Hyder Ali of Mysore. It is believed that his second name was "Jung", which means war, and it was later anglicised to Young. Hyder Hearsey was educated at Woolich. Due to the enforcement of the ban against the admission of Anglo-Indians into the Company's Army, he would have been denied Commission, but for the influence of his cousin Colonel Andrew Hearsey, Commandant of the Allahabad Fort. His first appointment was as aide-de-camp to the Nawab Wazir at Benares: he soon effected an exchange into the Mahratta service under Madhoji Scindia. In 1804 , Hyder Hearsey joined Lord Lake.

In the short War of 1971, several Anglo-Indian Airmen won Gallantry Awards.Air Marshal Maurice Barker,AVSM,Air Vice-Marshal J.F.Lazaro PVSM, J.J.Bouche AVSM and A.L.Michael AVSM,

Air Commodores Peter Motiland Wilson PVSM Mahavir Chakra, M.D.Wollan PVSM, Vernon Loyd PVSM, Group Captain Cecil Parker VM won the Mahavir Chakra for outstanding Gallantry and Vir Chakras were won by Group Captain Betry Weir, AVSM, Wing Commanders D.M.Conquest AVSM, Allen Alley and Squadron Leader D.Lazaro were awarded VMs and mentions in Despatches.

Lt. General Pat Dunn was awarded the Padma Bhushan, for his exceptional valour in the defence of his country, he took an active role in the Indo-Pakistan War in 1965.

Flight Lt. Bernard Owen Egan-Walker, was only 24 years old, when he was shot down in a bombing raid over Germany on the night of December 6th, 1944.

Air Marshall Denzil Keelor was commissioned in the I.A.F. on November 6th 1954.His career covered 36 years in the I.A.F. He had taken part in operations against Pakistan, in 1965 and 1971 and performed with distinctions. Denzil Keelor was awarded the Kirti

Chakra and the Vir Chakra by the President of India for Gallantry. Air
Marshal Denzil Keelor was born on the 7th December 1933. He is currently working as Advisor (Aviation) and is in charge of Certification and Inspection of Aircrew and Operational Surveillance, at the Directorate of Civil Aviation (DGCA).

The Battle of Kut, was another occasion when the courage of the Anglo-Indian soldiers was brought to the fore-front. The battle started in 1915 and lasted for one year. An Anglo-Indian battalion fought against the Turks in the River Tigris, near Kut, from 25th December 1915.The Turks over ran the position and only a third of the original force survived. Kut would have been captured on Christmas Day had the Anglo-Indian Battalion not stood their ground, according to General Townshend. Helen Rodriguez an Anglo-Indian girl from Bangalore won the George Medal Award for her courage and outstanding devotion to duty in the face of Japanese bombers at Taunggyi, Civil Hospital. Helen was Matron, stretcher-bearer and performed many operations.She was captured by the Chinese and then by the Japanese who thought she was a spy. Helen was bayoneted by a drunken Japanese soldier, but she survived all her ordeals at the P.O.W. camps.

85% of the women of the Women's Auxiliary Corps. of India (W.A.C) I, were Anglo-Indians. Apart from Nursing they also served in the Army and Navy Stores across the country.

Flight Lt. Warneford(1892-1950) of Bangalore was the first man to shoot down the first Zeppelin in France. He won the Victoria Cross and the Croix de Guerre.

After the Second World War sixteen Victoria Crosses were bestowed on Anglo-Indians and ninety-seven

Military Crosses were awarded for acts of heroism during the War.

Anglo-Indian History is not short of War Heroes and heroic deeds, with moments of defeat, valour and victory. Someone, somewhere should create A Virtual Anglo-Indian Cemetery in Cyberspace and on the Monument of the fallen Anglo-Indian soldier the following words of Thomas Arnold could be inscribed as an epitaph:

"Two things we ought to learn from History: One, that we are not in ourselves superior to our fathers; another, that we are shamefully and monstrously inferior to them, if we do not advance beyond them."

-T. Arnold

ANGLO-INDIAN LINKS

http://www.squidoo.com/melvynbrown

http://www.maxpages.com/theangloindian/

http://warrenbrown.tripod.com/angloindian/

http://www.squidoo.com/angloindians/

http://www.squidoo.com/advertising-a-race

http://greatest.knowledgehunter.ever.com/

http://www.squidoo.com/colonialbritishindiavide oshowcase

MODULE 11

BLOGGING ON THE WEB

Starting a Blog is a good method for expressing yourself on a variety of topics, for building a network of contacts, establishing yourself as an authority in the field of blogging and for promoting your own products and services. I would suggest that you start blogging by setting up your own blog on Blogger, Wordpress or Typepad. Below are a few of my Blog Entries, which I made some time ago, on a number of topics, which I was interested in, as well which were current at the time. It is an excellent idea to blog a lot about the top or hot searches on the major Search-Engines. This is one way for getting a lot of traffic, which consists of people who are interested in information related to the latest subjects in the news.

BLOG POSTS

Farrah Fawcett Passes Away: May Her Soul Rest in Peace!

An Angel on Earth Becomes An Angel in Heaven

Farrah Fawcett was a great personality, a great actress and a great inspiration for people all over the world. Everyone remembers the iconic "Charlie's Angel" television series. The world was surprised to know about Farah's cancer and her fight to overcome it.

Farrah Fawcett had an eventful career even doing a few serious roles and winning awards. I remember the posters of Farrah Fawcett growing up, with her stunning smile and down-to-earth presence. Almost every young man had a poster of Farrah Fawcett in his room.

It can rightly be said that Farrah Fawcett an Earth Angel, and she is now a Heavenly Angel. May Her Soul Rest in Peace.

http://warrenbrown.blogspot.com/2009_06_01_arc hive.html

When Will You be Famous?

There are a number of people who want to be rich and famous, almost 70 per cent of the world for that matter. Everyone who seeks fame is constantly in search of the right way to do things, to right places to be seen at, the right people to know and the right job or hobby to work act, in order to get noticed.

There are a number of ways to climb up the ladder of fame and success. We have a number of celebrities who have come from simple humble beginnings and who have then become superstars, in no time at all. The famous personalities who have made an impact in the world today and yesterday are in abundance. We have the superstars of yesteryear like Elvis Presley, Marilyn Monroe who are icons today, in the field of entertainment.

We have celebrities in all fields of endeavour, which could fill the pages of several volumes, with their famous quotes on all the aspects of life and love.

This brings us to the main question about, when will you be famous? The point is what would you have to do to be famous? To begin with, it would be a good idea to start blogging on a variety of topics which you feel strongly about. The next step would be to have a good User I.D. which is distinctive and unique, which you can use everywhere on the web for all the sites or blogs you create or for all the social network sites you join in, Facebook and Twitter, for example and for all the web forums you participate in. The third step is for you to create a You Tube account and upload a few videos on topics you are interested in. The fourth step for you to write a few articles and post them onto article websites, with a proper signature at the end which links back to your blog or website.The articles and the videos you have uploaded onto various sites, represent your Public Relations network, which works for you constantly sending people to your website and blog, while promoting you and your work worldwide, with a minimum investment into publicity.

The fifth and one of the most important steps for you to take is to write a book on a topic you are interested in, so that you can be an authority on the subject. Make sure to publicize your book, with free press releases, articles on blogs and websites and by participating in Forums, which are in your Niche of interest. Within a year, and if you keep constantly updating your Twitter, you will find that you will have over 1,000 followers who are interested in what you have to say.

I have found that it has helped having an I.D. like Warrenpeace21 on a variety of networks spread all across the web. The important point to keep in mind is that Fame does not come in a day, but after years of hard work and research. Make Fame your mission, and once you have acquired it and feel sick of it, make sure to hire a good Life Coach like myself, instead of ending your precious life like Elvis Presley, Marilyn Monroe, River Phoenix or Heath Ledger, tragic superstars, innocent victims of Fame and Success.

The Time for Gardening

Summer has finally arrived here in the United Kingdom. Avid Gardeners are now getting down on all fours and tending lovingly to their plants, whispering sweet-nothings as they plant the little saplings into the warm and nourishing earth.

A whole new range of plant products as well as summer products have now invaded the market. All these new and mostly old products are encouraging us to celebrate the season of summer, form gardening furniture and implements to the skin nourishing creams to protect us against the sunlight.

On Becoming the Romantic Book Hero

The women of this generation and over the last few generations have grown up reading romance novels, the Mills and Boon variety with great interest. Have the expectations of what women want in the ideal man changed due to the strong influence of the genre of the romantic novel? Literature has been a powerful medium of change over the centuries. Have romance novels changed the minds and the attitudes of women towards men for the better or for the worse?

When women search for the ideal man, do they search for the story book personalities which seem so perfect and romantic? The traits of the story book lover and hero is so exciting in the mind of the young school girl, who gradually transforms into the young lady, from the rebellious teenager at College and the strong-minded university student. The novel romantic hero is the type who is usually an outsider, a man with dark shadows lurking in his past, the man who is ready to protect his woman, the man who is blameless to the young woman he loves, the man who only can exist in the realm of the romance book.

What is the secret formula which is necessary for every novelist who sits down to create her romantic hero? The hero is an outsider who enters the world of the heroine, he turns her world upside down, saves her from the evils she has to face, vanquishes the villain who strives to capture her and then finally triumphs to have the fair lady in wrapped in his arms, as their world is bathed in the warmth of romantic glow and sunshine.

It may not be too long now before men start putting pen to paper and writing romantic novels through the male perspective. At least then men will have an idea about what it takes to become a romantic book hero who would appeal to every romantic woman who has grown up on a staple diet of romantic Mills and Boon novels.

http://warrenbrown.blogspot.com/2009_05_01_arc hive.html

Mum and Steven Seagal

My late Mum, Joan was a great fan of Steven Seagal. Mum liked to watch all Steven Seagal's movies and thought that he was a great action movie star. Mum would say that she liked Steven Seagal because he was always very cool when he would confront the bad guys and you would never see him losing his temper.

I remember the first time we saw Steven Seagal movie, it was in "Under Siege" in 1992, where he is a cook on a battleship and confronts the villains in the forms of Gary Busey and Tommy Lee Jones, not forgetting the beautiful, "Birthday Cake Girl" semi-nude Erika Eleniak. This was a great movie and made a big impression on the four of us, Mum, Dad, my sister and myself.

Although Steven Seagal is a tall and imposing figure he moves like a cat and takes on the villains like they were flies. The actor himself is very interested in the Martial arts and is quite proficient in the Eastern Arts of meditation.

In life we need to be able to confront our challenges with a calm and peaceful mind and to be aware of the fact that every situation changes. We do not need to battle our way through life, but to be able to calmly move them aside effortlessly. This state of mind where we react calmly to life situations can be achieved if we learn to practise meditation and understand the life is always teaching us to improve ourselves.

In the movies, Steven Seagall takes on the bad guys and tosses them around. We do not need to do this in life. We need to control our tempers and our tongues, while concentrating our mind on inner peace of mind. As we practise the art of the mind warrior we will learn how to overcome our own fears and weaknesses, we will gradually understand that life has great rewards to offer to those who understand the value of life, with all its joys, sorrows, victories and defeats.

Steven Seagal has made a number of movies since "Under Siege". A few of his other movies are "Under Siege 2", "On Deadly Ground", "Above the Law", "Marked for Death", "Cradle to the Grave", being just a few of them. Take the time to get a Steven Seagal movie to watch today and appreciate the value of the character he portrays on screen.

Why Blogging is so important?

A blog helps a writer to express his thoughts to the world.

A blog helps a person to express his views on a variety of topics.

A Niche Blog focuses on a particular topic. There are blogs on advertising, fishing, photography and on every topic you can imagine.

Bloggers and Blogging is one of the best phenomenon on the web.

http://warrenbrown.blogspot.com/2008_07_01_arc hive.html

MODULE 12

THE SQUIDOO FACTOR

Ways to Earn Money on Squidoo

1. Use the Text link adverts: Chitika ads
2. Use the Text link adverts: InfoLinks
3. Google Adsense which appears on all pages
4. Display adverts- The Beebo ad bar(trial)
5. Amazon product module
6. EBay product module
7. Café Press product module
8. Etsy product module
9. Zazzle product module
10. Advertise your own product or service

11. Affiliate product links, to which you belong, like Clickbank.

THE SQUIDOO MONEYMAKING NETWORK

I thoroughly enjoy creating sites or lens on Squidoo. A Squidoo site is an ecommerce site in itself. You can make a Squidoo lens on any topic of your choice, and as many lens as you wish. There is a powerful Ecommerce feature, on Squidoo, which displays all the products related to the theme feature on your site.

When people come to read the content of your site, and find products related to the theme, they tend to buy an item or two. When this happens, you earn some money, either for yourself or for a Charity of your choice.

The money you have earned is then sent to you to your Pay Pal account, or to the Charity of your choice, once your account has reached the payout limit. You will also have the opportunity of becoming a Giant Squid, if you have completed more than 50 successful Lens on Squidoo. This is yet another powerful method for getting your Expert credentials in your field, for earning money and for driving traffic to your site.

TITLES OF SQUIDOO LENS
WITH THEIR URLS

Advertising Making Money with Newsroom
http://www.squidoo.com/moneynewsroom/

Advertising Mini Course on Squidoo
http://www.squidoo.com/advertisingcourse/

Advertising the Disappearing Anglo-Indian community
http://www.squidoo.com/advertising-a-race/

Affiliate KB (Knowledge Base): Guide to Affiliate Marketing
http://www.squidoo.com/affiliateknowledge/

Affiliate Marketing Gurus Today
http://www.squidoo.com/affiliategurus/

Become a Virtual Entrepreneur, Webpreneur with Low Investment
http://www.squidoo.com/webpreneur/

Bruce Lee Video Showcase on Squidoo

http://www.squidoo.com/bruceleevideos/

Bruce Willis Video Showcase on Squidoo
http://www.squidoo.com/brucewillisvideoshowcase/

Christmas Gifts Video Showcase
http://www.squidoo.com/christmasgiftsvideoshowcase/

Comedy Video Showcase on Squidoo
http://www.squidoo.com/comedyvideoshowcase/

Ebooks Video Showcase on Squidoo
http://www.squidoo.com/ebooksvideoshowcase/

Einstein on Squidoo
http://www.squidoo.com/geniuseinstein/

Elvis Video Showcase
http://www.squidoo.com/elvistheking/

Enculturation
http://www.squidoo.com/enculturation/

Entrepreneurs Video Showcase on Squidoo
http://www.squidoo.com/entrepreneursvideos/

Fame Video Showcase on Squidoo
http://www.squidoo.com/famevideo/

Famous Supermodels Video Showcase on Squidoo
http://www.squidoo.com/supermodelvideoshow/

Genealogy,Family History and Ancestry
http://www.squidoo.com/ancestralgenealogy/

Hollywoodmovies Video Showcase on Squidoo
http://www.squidoo.com/hollywoodmoviesvideos
howcase/

How to be a Writer and an Author
http://www.squidoo.com/makingauthors/

How to get Rich and Famous Independently! On
Squidoo http://www.squidoo.com/richfame/

Immigration Video Showcase on Squidoo
http://www.squidoo.com/immigrationvideoshowc
ase/

Inculturation
http://www.squidoo.com/inculturation/

Inspector Closeau Video Showcase on Squidoo
http://www.squidoo.com/inspectorcloseauvideosh
owcase/

Internet Marketing Video Showcase on Squidoo
http://www.squidoo.com/internetmarketingvids/

Jesus on Squidoo
http://www.squidoo.com/christjesus/

King Arthur Video Showcase on Squidoo

http://www.squidoo.com/kingarthurvideoshowcase/

Libraries Video Showcase on Squidoo
http://www.squidoo.com/librariesvideoshowcase/

Life Coaching Video Showcase on Squidoo
http://www.squidoo.com/lifecoachingvideoshowcase/

Making Profits with More Niche! On Squidoo
http://www.squidoo.com/profitniche/

Melvyn Brown, Anglo-Indian Chronicler on Squidoo
http://www.squidoo.com/melvynbrown/

Mother Teresa of Calcutta on Squidoo
http://www.squidoo.com/motherteresa/

Nicholas Hammond Spiderman Video Showcase
http://www.squidoo.com/nicholashammondspidermanvideoshowcase/

Paul McKenna Video Showcase on Squidoo
http://www.squidoo.com/paulmckennavideoshowcase/

Pyramids Video Showcase on Squidoo

http://www.squidoo.com/pyramidsvideoshowcase
/

Rudyard Kipling stories Video Showcase
http://www.squidoo.com/rudyardkiplingstoriesvi
deoshowcase/

Secret of Eternal Youth
http://www.squidoo.com/youngforever/

Tarzan the King of the Jungle!
http://www.squidoo.com/kingtarzan/

Tarzan Video Showcase
http://www.squidoo.com/tarzanbyedgarriceburro
ughsvideoshowcase/

The Secret Race: Anglo-Indians
http://www.squidoo.com/angloindians/

Tracking down the World's Greatest Detectives
http://www.squidoo.com/detectives/

Warren Brown: The Greatest Knowledge Hunter
Ever: On Squidoo
http://greatest.knowledgehunter.ever.com/

Web Millionaires Video Showcase
http://www.squidoo.com/webmillionairesvideosh
owcase/

Wedding Video Showcase
http://www.squidoo.com/weddingvideoshowcas/

Wild West Movies
http://www.squidoo.com/wildwestvideos/

Wild West Movies Video Showcase on Squidoo
http://www.squidoo.com/wildwestmovies/

Wild West Vids Video Showcase on Squidoo
http://www.squidoo.com/wildwestvidsvideoshow
case/

World War II Videos Video Showcase on Squidoo
http://www.squidoo.com/worldwariivideosvideos
howcase/

MODULE 13

VIDEO MARKETING

SUCCESS VIDEOS ON YOU TUBE

Promote your Cause, your talent and your skills on You
Tube. I have made a collection of Videos on the
Success Niche and on the Anglo-Indian Niche. I have
given the links below. You Tube is very popular, and so

it gets a large amount of traffic of people who are interested in a variety of topics. Everyone can become a Star with a large fan following on You Tube, if you happen to have an exceptional talent. Start with something simple, unique and special and before long you will find that your video will receive tonnes of traffic. Make sure to spread the word around about your new videos, using Facebook, Twitter, your blogs and sites.

SUCCESS VIDEOS

Secret Recipe for Success!

Do you possess the right ingredients to make a success of your life?

You have all the skills and the talents necessary to make your life a success, only you are not aware of it.

Ask Warren, the Success Coach for guidance today.

http://www.youtube.com/watch?v=Y6lkxWp---o

Secret Formula for Success!

Do you have the secret formula for Success?

Do you want to Succeed?

Are you willing to pay to do a course for success?

Are you willing to become an Affiliate with minimal investment?

http://www.youtube.com/watch?v=XwsHhZ0G_p0

Unlimited Success!

What is Unlimited Success and how can you get it?

Unlimited success is the type of success that you can achieve with guidance and planning from a person who believes in Success and who will be willing to help you to succeed.

http://www.youtube.com/watch?v=GMGdzLAZyFo

Success motivators!

Do you have your Success motivators?

Do you feel successful every day?

You can be a Success, if you believe you can.

You can become the Richest person in the world, if you believe you can.

http://www.youtube.com/watch?v=LLeEwhb3lPo

Secret of the Success Book

In this video you will learn about the Secret of the Success book.

Do you keep a notebook?

Do you write down your ideas?

Do you have a million dollar idea?

Yes, you may have and lost one, if you have not written it down.

http://www.youtube.com/watch?v=GhsYZ6CSTfg

Success Moment by Warren

Warren helps you to discover your Success Moment.

Your Success Moment is the time when you discover that great idea which will make you a fortune.

Do not lose that SUCCESS MOMENT.

http://www.youtube.com/watch?v=796J6QxCAc8

Learn Success

Warren Brown on You Tube speaks about Learning Success and how we can all be successful.

http://www.youtube.com/watch?v=hhwCNkmsp
Us

MODULE 14

FAME AND FORTUNE NICHE
IN INTERNET MARKETING

1. **Your Fame and Success Blueprint:** You need
   to create your own Fame and Success Blueprint.
   Begin by writing all your goals and objectives.
   Ask yourself a few questions. How Rich do you
   want to be? How Famous do you want to be?
   What will you do with all your Wealth and
   Fame? Are you willing to work towards making

your own fame and fortune? What motivates you and what inspires you?

2. **Your Centre-of-Operations:** Get a spot in your room or your home office, where you can set up your Centre-of-Operations. Put up your charts, plans, strategies and all that inspires you to go forth for your fame and fortune. Set up your computer, files, reference books and all that you will need close by for your new venture.

3. **Your Product or service:** Create a product or service around something which you have a great interest or passion.

4. **Affiliates:** If you sell your digital products on the web, and you sell them on Commission Junction, Clickbank or Pay dot com, you will have a number of Affiliates who will sell your products. It is important for you to have good offers, and special offers to keep your affiliates happy.

5. **Your Website and Blog:** Get your own dot com website and blog. It is important to get an appropriate name for your own dot com, dot org or dot net site which reflects your business.

6. **Branding:** Create your Brand on the web. Your brand should represent what you sell, your business, services and products.

7. **Social Network sites:** Join Facebook, Twitter, Linkedin and promote your work and build your contact list.

8. **Article Marketing:** Join article sites, like Ezine articles, Helium, Hubpages and Triond. Submit your articles on various topics or topics related to your Niche.

9. **Search Engine Optimization:** Use the WEB CEO program to submit your links to several websites. Do this on a regular basis.

10. **You Tube Marketing:** Make a couple of videos related to your product, service and Niche. Spread the word and watch your popularity grow.

11. **Press Release:** Join a few paid and free Press Release sites on the web, to promote your business.

12. **Book Publishing:** Write a book related to your product or service. Your book can contain most of your articles which you had submitted to several article sites on the web.

13. **Affiliate Marketing:** To enter the field of Affiliate Marketing, which means to sell other people's products or services, you will need to join a few sites like Amazon, Clickbank and Paydotcom as an Affiliate member. You will earn commissions on all sales made for the products which you promote on your websites or blogs.

14. **EZine publishing:** Publish your own Ezine or join a site like Openzine and create your own specialized ezine around your Niche.

15. **Mailing List:** Start building your own Mailing list to promote your product. Offer advice and free products in order to build trust and to establish yourself as an Expert in your field.

16. **Newsletter:** Send out a weekly or monthly newsletter to keep your Customers informed about your business and the release of new products or services. A good Autoresponder for your Marketing list is also essential like AWeber. An Autoresponder is an automated system, which send out mailings at specified times to your loyal email or course and membership subscribers.

17. **Product Launches:** A Product Launch can be done online or offline. Make sure to create a state of interest among your customers for your new product, in this way you ensure the success of your latest product.

18. **Advertising and Publicity:** The Media is very important for your enterprise. Prepare and keep a Media kit ready. The Media kit should contain information about you, your business and your products and services.

19. **Trends, styles and the web:** In order to be a success in the online and offline world of commerce, it is essential to be aware of all the customers changing trends, tastes and styles. In this way, you will need to come out with new and innovative ways for creating and promoting your products and services.

20. **Public Speaking:** Visit local schools, colleges and clubs in your area and speak about your subject. This will establish you as an authority in your field. People will want to buy your products and services, thus helping you on the road to riches and fame.

21. **Community work:** Donate to local causes, once you are successful in the community. This is also one way of getting social recognition in the real world as well for the promotion of your business in the local community. Participate in community work and you can be sure that the community will come forward to support you in our ventures.

MODULE 15

ARTICLE MARKETING ON HUBPAGES

Hubs are articles on the Hubpages dot com website. I have a number of my articles published on Hubpages. I have included the two given below, which are related to being Famous. I also get a lot of traffic from Hubpages, to my websites and blogs. Take my advice and start creating your Hubs today.

Elements of Celebrity-hood

When ordinary people do extraordinary things in the public eye, they enter the realm of Celebrity hood. In some cases this is purely by chance, in some it is after a long struggle, while with others, it is the result of careful planning and by getting to know the right people. While some people achieve fame and fortune by being in the right place at the right time and by doing the right thing to get noticed, others need to develop a strategy to attain fame, fortune and success.

The media makes the celebrity. When a person becomes famous, he or she is automatically put into the spotlight by the media. The new celebrity's life is taken over by the media, which prints articles about the life of the celebrity, in every national and international newspaper and magazine. Advertisement campaigns are launched and the celebrity is also the Brand Ambassador for many brand names. A good test of a Celebrity's fame is when he or she is in demand. It is not easy or cheap to get good publicity from the media. On the other hand it is the life of the celebrity and of other celebrities which keep the media in business.

There are also cases of several new celebrities who cannot handle their fame and fortune. These types of people, without proper mentors, go into drugs, drink and sex, gradually being featured in all media publications, broadcasts and announcements for making the news for all the wrong reasons. This is an instance where the media can break the celebrity, eventually resulting in the decline of the star celebrity.

The Elements of Celebrity-hood are given below:

1. Charisma, popularity and a magnetic personality

2. A good relationship with the Media

3. A good Manager who can manage the business and the Celebrity

4. Well planned Promotional Campaigns

5. An Agent who keeps bringing the best jobs in.

6. A good Life Coach who can keep the Celebrity focussed and on the right path.

7. Creating a positive Media Image.

8. Building of a strong Brand Image.

9. Sound Financial Investments.

10. Creation of new Brands, Products and the introduction of new ideas into the program.

11. Being in the company of the right type of people

12. Writing a good inspirational Autobiography

13. Contributing to Charities and good causes

14. Social networking, blogging and the development of a good website

15. Remembering the Fans who made you a Celebrity

How to be a Dynamic Success?

Think Success: If you think Success you can be a Success.

How can we think Success?

These are a few of the ways in which you could think Success.

You can think Success by reading about those who have been a Success.

You can think Success by hearing those who are a Success.

You can think Success by studying those who are a Success.

You can think Success by following the Success Blueprints of those who are a Success.

Develop a Success Mindset

A Success Mindset is when a person creates a very success oriented way of thinking. Can anyone develop such a Success Mindset?

Yes, anyone can develop such a Success Mindset, with a little planning and effort.

Success Motivators For Success

Nothing Succeeds Like Success!

A Man without Dreams is like a bird with broken wings!

Make things happen, do not wait for things to happen.

There is no limit to Your Success!

Make Success A Way of Life!

Eat, Drink and Live Success!

Make Success your Friend by spending more time creating it.

Success is not Luck, but the result of the Success Mindset.

Plan Your Success One Day at a Time.

Time is Money and Time is Success.

If you have ten skills you have ten reasons to be a Success!

Your Ten Skills are Ten Successful Moneymaking Streams of Income.

The World Wants YOU to be a Success Today!

Figure Out Your Priorities

We all have a long list of Priorities which we need to fulfil in life. This list of Priorities, which range from family to career, personal goals and objectives in life, which are in turn linked to our values and ethics in life. These priorities become ingrained into our personalities over a period of time. The point is do you have the right set of priorities, or do you need to re-arrange them, so that you and everyone around you can benefit from your work.

How do you make your List of Priorities? This is just a shortlist, but you will need to sit down and create your own list in order to make the necessary changes and improvements in your life.

List of Priorities

1. **Family**

(a) Spouse

(b) Children

(c) Parents

(d)Grandparents

(e) Relatives and In-laws

2. Career

(a) Boss

(b) Colleagues

(c) Projects

(d) Responsibilities

(e) Career advancement

(f) Skills for the workplace

3. Friends

(a) Spending time with Friends

(b) Keeping in touch by emailing

(c) Joining a Club

(d) Showing an interest in your friends

4. Hobbies and Interests

(a) Finding new hobbies
(b) Developing old hobbies

(c) Doing a bit of research on the web related to your hobbies.

1. Skill development
(a) What skills do you lack in life?

(b) Find new challenges, which is an excuse to develop new skills.

2. Other interests
(a) Religion

(b) Art

(c) Music

(d) Books

(e) Cinema

MODULE 16

INTERNET MARKETING FAME AND FORTUNE PROGRAMS

We all want to get rich and famous but how many
of us really try to do so.
Those who try never stop till they are successful.
There are those who are not sure about what to do.
There are those who are misled by people with false
promises.

Where do you fit in?

Are you the type of person who needs to be guided
to the right places to do the job on your own?

Are you the type of person, who needs someone
else to do the job for you, as you are too busy with
all your daily work and obligations and have no time
to concentrate on getting rich and famous.

Your regular job is not going to make you famous
and rich. If your present job will make you rich and
famous, then you have no reason to read this book.
In that case I would suggest that you gift this book
to a good friend, who can benefit from the research
and advice, as well as practical advice which this

book has to offer, by a person who is also moving towards fame and success.

BELIEVE IN YOURSELF!

BELIEVE THAT YOU ARE ON THE PATH TO FAME AND WEALTH!

There is a wealth of information in the world today. We only need to look in the right places to find what we need, in order to change our lives and to have a richer and more popular existence.

There is enough wealth in the world for everyone.

Everyone has a right to the Wealth in the World.

You have that Right for Wealth and Success Too.

http://www.publishsuccess.com
http://warrenbrown.tripod.com/blog

Rich and Famous Programs

1. Greasy Palm
2. FREE Stock Market Wealth Building Course
3. Brand YOU!
4. Create a Rich List

5. Go Thunk Yourself
6. Easy Money Reviews
7. Springboard to Stardom
8. Your Famous People Address Bible
9. How to Get Rich and Famous from Your Job-Blog
10. Linguistics to Fame and Wealth
11. This Company creates Tons of Millionaires
12. Get A Famous Entrepreneur Mentor!
13. Secrets of World Famous Entrepreneurs, Are Yours FREE
14. FREE Advertising for Wealth and Fame
15. Duplicate the Secrets of Wealthy People
16. Get Rich on the Internet in 7 Easy Steps
17. Self Promotion to Wealth and Success
18. Broadcast Yourself to Wealth and Fame
19. AFFILIATION for Profit
20. Your First Blog
21. Discover the Power of Forum Networking
22. Create Your Product and Your Brand
23. Market Yourself and your Product

1. Greasy Palm
Greasy Palm is a website that Pays You to Shop!
On joining this website You Earn £2.50 for FREE.
Then get £171.25 for Special Offers!
Refer a Friend and Earn £7.00

URL OF Greasy Palm
http://www.greasypalm.co.uk/index.php

2. Stock Market Wealth Building

You can be Rich if you know How the Stock
Market works.

Make a Fortune with Winning Stock Market Secrets!
JOIN the FREE Stock Market Course!

URL of Win Investing
http://WinInvesting.co.uk

3. Brand You!

Create Your Own Brand!

This is an essential Key to Fame, Fortune and Success.
Market yourself and your Talents.
What better way, than having your own dot com.
To be a Brand Success, with minimal expense, get Your Own Domain.

4. Create a Rich List

Create Your Own Rich List which you can always refer to when you have to send out your party invitations.

Get Hollywood Celebrity Addresses.

Use these addresses to send out Complimentary gifts and Congratulatory notes to the Superstars when they have something to celebrate about. Chances are, the Stars will not send you a note, you may get an autograph if you are lucky or the Stars Secretary may mail you a letter on behalf of the celebrity. Collect these souvenirs, it all helps in the long-term.

URL of Hollywood Celebrity Addresses

http://www.hollywoodusa.co.uk/celebrity-homes.htm

5. Thunk Wealth and Success!

Follow this simple 14-Day Online Plan to become Rich, Famous and a Success on your own.

URL of the Thunk Blog:

http://gothunkyourself.blogspot.com/

6. Easy Money Reviews

This website has a list of genuine sites on which you can earn money in the fastest possible time.

Get Your FREE Information Today!

URL of Easy Money Reviews:

http://easymoneyreviews.co.uk/index.html

7. Springboard to Stardom!

Join the Springboard Program FREE.

Your Springboard to become A Star!

Take part in Acting Auditions.

Check out Great Modelling Opportunities.

Springboard UK URL:

http://www.pm-global-services.com/indexauditions.php

8. Your Famous People Address Bible

Get the Addresses of Famous Movie, Television and Music Stars, popular in the United States and the United Kingdom.

Build Your Famous People Hot-List and get their attention with the help of souvenirs, photos, articles. Do not harass these Stars as they are people too and need their privacy.

The Hot-List URL:

http://www.addressbible.com/

9. How to Get Rich and Famous from Your Job-Blog.

In this strategy to get Rich and Famous you create a blog about your job and spice it with nuggets of curious incidents and characters, with novel insights to make it popular.

Do not overdo the revelations on your job front, or you could be sacked if your boss found out, as it has happened in a number of cases in the past. Be a cautious and creative blogger.

You can monetize (Earn money) your blog, with Google Adsense.

URL to Job Blog Fame:

http://internetslacker.livejournal.com/2680.html

10. How to Get Rich and Famous with Linguistics?

This is an interesting article with valuable insights into the art of getting rich with the help of Linguistics, especially if you have a ear for languages. This article was prepared by Sophia Malamud.

URL for rich Linguistics:

http://www.ling.upenn.edu/advice/rnf/

11. How to Become Stupid Rich?

This Company is creating Millionaires, Are You Next?

Do you want to have endless cash and a lifestyle for people to envy?

Money Does Grow On Trees, if you know where to look.

Join Profitmatic, Your Automated Internet Profit Centre.

URL for Profitmatic:

http://solution4life.profitmatic.com/

12. Get A Famous Entrepreneur Mentor!

Learn the skills from a famous Entrepreneur.

The 8 Essential Secrets for entrepreneur information.
Chris Cardell is Britain's leading Expert on Entrepreneural Business Success.

URL for Your Entrepreneur Mentor:

http://www.EntrepreneurEssentials.co.uk

13. Famous Entrepreneurs Teach You Success!

Learn the useful skills and strategies for achieving Wealth and Fame from Famous Entrepreneurs down the ages, like Benjamin Franklin, Ben and Jenny, William Penn, Bill Gates, Eli Whitney, Oprah Winfrey and others.

URL of the Famous Entrepreneurs:

http://entrepreneurs.about.com/od/famousentrepreneurs/

14. Advertise Your Brand and Your Product FREE!

Join Craigslist and Post your advertisements for FREE.

Post Classifieds for Jobs, Apartments, Personals, For Sale, Services, Community and Events.

Do something Creative and Innovative. Announce it to the World with the help of Craigslist.

URL of Craigslist:

http://london.craigslist.org/

15. Duplicate Wealth and Success!

Get the Secrets of Success from the Wealthy People of Society.
Learn, Practise and Duplicate their methods of Wealth and fame building, from their Videos, Biographies, as well as from the articles of wealthy men and women.

URL to Duplicate Wealth and Success:

http://www.secretsofsuccess.com

16. How to Get Rich on the Internet in 7 Easy Steps?

This is a valuable article with a lot of useful nuggets of information to guide you on your way to Wealth and Fame. This article was written by Michael J. McGroarty, and was published on the Webpronews website.
URL to get rich Online in 7 Easy Steps:

http://www.webpronews.com/topnews/2001/10/28/how-to-get-rich-on-the-internet-in-easy-steps

17. Self Promotion to Wealth and Success!

Promote Your website for FREE, on this website.

Showcase your talents for the World.

Create your own online Portfolio.

URL to Self-Promotion:

http://www.freebyte.com/free_website_promotio/

18. Broadcast Yourself to Wealth and Fame!

Record Yourself on Video in Action, whether it is dancing, singing, talking, acting or just working, upload it to You Tube and watch yourself get a fan following in no time at all.

URL for You Tube Success:

http://www.youtube.com

19. AFFILIATION to Wealth and Profit

Web Affiliation is a great concept of selling the Products of other people for Profit.

You can sell these products by pasting HTML code on your website. Whenever a person buys a product from the Company, using your website, you earn a commission. These commissions can add up to a substantial gain in the long term.

To check out some great Affiliate Programs you can visit the websites of Clickbank, Commission Junction and Amazon.

http://warrenbiz.dayjobkill.hop.clickbank.net/

http://warrenbiz.paidetc.hop.clickbank.net/

http://warrenbiz.surveyis.hop.clickbank.net/

http://warrenbiz.xoftspyse.hop.clickbank.net/

http://warrenbiz.salehoo.hop.clickbank.net/

http://warrenbiz.bryxen4.hop.clickbank.net/

http://warrenbiz.1free.hop.clickbank.net/

http://warrenbiz.spywarebot.hop.clickbank.net/

http://warrenbiz.secretaff.hop.clickbank.net/

http://warrenbiz.bryxen1.hop.clickbank.net/

http://astore.amazon.com/warrbrowlitee-20

http://www.EBookGold.com/index/cashman

http://www.mylot.com/?ref=warrenbrown

http://cbglobe.com/x.cgi?id=warren6

http://www.otogoldmine.com/21291/go

20. Your First Blog

Create your First Blog and make it a habit to write something on your blog everyday. Write about everyday things in your own style and before long you will have fans and they will be willing to buy your products.

http://publishsuccess.vox.com

http://blog.myspace.com/warrenwriter

21. Discover the Power of Forum Networking

Join a Forum and get famous every time you leave a message. People who read your message will want to know more about you, which will make them click on your profile to view your details, which is where you give your web address.

Forum Networking is a very powerful way to get more people to view your site, buy your products and in a way to also make you known as a writer and an Expert in your field.

http://www.webproworld.com

http://www.conqueryourniche.com

22. Create your Product and Your Brand

Make your websites, as many as you can handle.
Promote yourself, your Company and Your
Products.
Create your Products, whether it is a collection of
Photographs, e-books or articles on a certain niche
like Animal care, stamp collecting or fishing.

Advertise Your Product and Your Brand and before
long you will have your own Brand Image and a
valuable information product to go with it if you do
not have a tangible one.

23. Market yourself and your Product

It pays to advertise.

Advertise your site on several search-engines like Google, MSN, Lycos and Yahoo.

Organize workshops on your area of Expertise.

Give Lectures on your particular subject.

Publish Books on your topic and become an Expert.

CONGRATULATIONS

YOU ARE NOW ON YOUR WAY
TO BECOMING
A SNOW STORM
MARKETING GRADUATE
INDEPENDENTLY

SNOW STORM MARKETING RESOURCES

Social Sites

Facebook- www.facebook.com
Twitter- www.twitter.com
Bebo- www.bebo..com
Twellow- www.twellow.com
Linkedin- http://linkedin.com

Social Bookmarks

Digg- http://digg.com
Del.icio.us- http://del.icio.us
Stumbleupon- www.stumbleupon.com
Technorati- http://technorati.com
Share This- www.sharethis.com

Networks

Ning- www.ning.com
Start Up- www.startup.ning.com
Sokule: www.sokule.com
Social Spark- http://socialspark.com

News Network

Newsvine- www.newsvine.com

Blogs

http://warrenbrown.wordpress.com/
http://publishsuccess.vox.com/
http://warrenbrown.tripod.com/blog
http://my.telegraph.co.uk/warrenpeace21/
http://blog.myspace.com/warrenwriter
http://warrenpeace21.spaces.live.com
http://www.blogcatalog.com/user/Wordsmith
http://warrenbrown21.tripod.com/blog
http://www.webon.com
http://www.blog-search.com

http://www.express.co.uk
http://www.thoughts.com/Warrenpeace21
Press Releases
http://www.freepressreleases.co.uk
http://www.speedypr.com
http://www.greatreporter.com
http://www.free-press-release.com/
http://www.pressexposure.com

Self Publishing

Lulu- www.lulu.com
Create Space- www.createspace.com
You Publish- www.youpublish.com

Video Marketing

http://video.google.com/
http://current.com/
http://youtube.com/
http://www.virginmediashorts.co.uk
http://www.livevideo.com/
http://www.tubemogul.com

Internet Marketing

http://www.startupcommunity.co.uk/
http://www.linkreferral.com
http://www.freeaddepot.com
http://www.craigslist.org
http://www.thewidgeteers.com
http://www.mogulus.com/TheWidgeteers
http://www.theleaderworld.com
http://daily.mequoda.com/

Forum

http://webproworld.com

Search Engine Optimization Software

http://www.webceo.com/

Article Directories

http://www.amazines.com
http://www.articlealley.com
http://www.ezinearticles.com
http://www.1888articles.com

Affiliate Programs

www.linkshare.com
www.moreniche.com
www.tradedoubler.com
www.implix.com
www.paydotcom.com/
http://affiliate-program.amazon.co.uk
http://astore.amazon.com/warrbrowlitee-20
http://astore.amazon.co.uk/warrbrowlitee-21
http://www.affiliateguide.com
http://www.commissionjunction.com
http://www.clickbank.com
http://www.cbglobe.com
http://www.click2sell.eu

Email Marketing

http://www.constantcontact.com/
http://www.verticalresponse.com/
http://www.aweber.com

ABOUT WARREN BROWN

Warren Brown is a freelance writer, copywriter and Life Coach, specializing in creating effective copy and informative research articles. Warren Brown has published several books and he has been actively involved in the field of Internet Marketing and publishing since 1998.

http://www.publishsuccess.com

http://www.positivewriting.com

http://www.lulu.com/warrenmelvynbrown

http://warrenbrown.tripod.com/angloindian

http://cbglobe.com/x.cgi?id=warren6

http://astore.amazon.com/warbrowlitee-20

http://lifecoach4.tripod.com/blog

http://warrenbrown.tripod.com/freedreams

ISBN 978-1-4457-3683-9
NOTES

NOTES